T0147778

The Real Estate Buyer's Awareness Plan

The Ten Basic Steps to Find and Buy That "Just Right" Property

Joseph J. Pacelli

EXCLUSIVE BUYER'S AGENT
Licensed Real Estate Broker
New Jersey—Florida

STATE CERTIFIED GENERAL CONTRACTOR

iUniverse, Inc.
Bloomington

The Real Estate Buyer's Awareness Plan
The Ten Basic Steps to Find and Buy That "Just Right" Property

Copyright © 2011 by JNJ REALTY LLC

All rights reserved. No part of this book may be used or reproduced by any means, graphic, electronic, or mechanical, including photocopying, recording, taping or by any information storage retrieval system without the written permission of JNJ REALTY LLC. except in the case of brief quotations embodied in critical articles and reviews.

This publication has been assembled from information available to the public through various sources including, but not limited to, radio, TV, Internet, printed material, trade journals, current events, and knowledge obtained through personal experiences.

This publication is designed to provide information, on the subject matter presented, to the general public and should not be used in place of professional legal advice.

iUniverse books may be ordered through booksellers or by contacting:

iUniverse
1663 Liberty Drive
Bloomington, IN 47403
www.iuniverse.com
1-800-Authors (1-800-288-4677)

Because of the dynamic nature of the Internet, any web addresses or links contained in this book may have changed since publication and may no longer be valid. The views expressed in this work are solely those of the author and do not necessarily reflect the views of the publisher, and the publisher hereby disclaims any responsibility for them.

Any people depicted in stock imagery provided by Thinkstock are models, and such images are being used for illustrative purposes only.

Certain stock imagery © Thinkstock.

ISBN: 978-1-4620-0040-1 (sc)
ISBN: 978-1-4620-0041-8 (dj)
ISBN: 978-1-4620-0042-5 (ebook)

Library of Congress Control Number: 2011903392

Printed in the United States of America

iUniverse rev. date: 03/25/2011

Why Do You Need This Home Buyer's Handbook?

Are you:

*confused by the home buying process?
*terrified by all the horrible stories?
*unsure if you can make a purchase?
*unaware of your credit score?
*looking for a starter home?
*a first-time buyer?
*trying to downsize?
*ready for a "fixer upper"?
*unfamiliar with the Law of Agency?
*a SERIOUS BUYER?

If you answered *yes to any or all of the above, you should use this Home Buyer's Handbook to make that "just right" real estate purchase.*

DON'T GO SHOPPING WITHOUT IT!!

Dedicated to all you

SERIOUS HOME BUYERS

"HANG IN THERE"

The housing market will make a comeback.

When it happens, will you be ready, willing,
and able to make the right moves?

AWARENESS IS THE BUYER'S EDGE

YES!

YOU CAN BUY A HOME

YOUR ADVENTURE

IS ABOUT TO BEGIN

HAPPY HUNTING!

Preface

My purpose for making these few thoughts and comments available to potential home buyers is to assist them as they attempt to locate and buy that "just right" property.

I did not have much guidance when I started out looking for my first purchase. I had to learn and become AWARE of all the dangers on my own. However, I must say that I was fortunate enough not to get into too much trouble. I survived.

If those people, who find themselves in serious financial trouble, would have had the benefit of my knowledge and experience, they would not have overextended themselves. They would not have been lured into accepting that easy-to-obtain "low down payment" or in fact, that "no down payment," mortgage loan. I am certain that there would be fewer defaults and foreclosures.

I believe that anyone trying to purchase a home in today's market needs to be very familiar with the challenges that lie ahead.

You must be very careful. It's a jungle out there! Just follow the Ten Basic Steps To Find And Buy "That Just Right Property".

Joseph J Pacelli

STEP ONE

Learn the language of real estate and the Law of Agency

STEP TWO

Do you know who is on your side and looking out for you?

STEP THREE

Organize a viable plan before you start the searching phase.

STEP FOUR

Are you familiar with the three famous words of wisdom?

STEP FIVE

You should develop an advanced level of *AWARENESS*.

STEP SIX

You must make all the arrangements for your financing ASAP.

STEP SEVEN

Understand how to establish and apply true market value.

STEP EIGHT

Prepare yourself to negotiate for the best possible deal.

STEP NINE

Gain the confidence you need to become a stronger buyer.

STEP TEN

Now comes the best part, the closing: *The American Dream.*

Acknowledgments

To my mother, who encouraged me at an early age to get involved in the real estate business. She always believed in home ownership as part of THE AMERICAN DREAM. And, so do I!

To my father, who guided me through the many challenges of the construction business. He had a way of teaching me, by example, a very strong work ethic. He would say, "Get your hands dirty. It won't hurt you. It will be good for you." And, looking back, he was right.

To my wife, who has worked with me through the many ups and downs of the real estate business. To this day, she is still saying, "Hang in there."

To my son, who took my advice and bought his first house, a "fixer-upper". He turned it into a home that he is proud to own, and, I might add, not a bad investment.

To my pal Squiggs, a.k.a. TJ, who offered some very innovative suggestions that were inserted into the finished manuscript.

INTRODUCTION

Welcome aboard. Take this cruise on the truly exciting adventure of

FINDING+BUYING+OWNING

that "just right" dream home. The one you will enjoy calling your own.

Real estate ownership will continue to be the best, and generally the most secure, short term and long term investment for the average growing family.

Home ownership is still the best way, and usually the only way, for most families to build solid equity and attain long term financial security. The history of the real estate market has proven that property values most often appreciate in the long run. However, in the event the real estate market does turn cold, property values can plunge quickly. It happens almost overnight and usually without any advanced notice.

THERE ARE NO GUARANTEES

Nevertheless, with sound acquired knowledge and careful planning, The Ten Basic Steps To Find And Buy That Just Right Property will guide you safely through the mine fields and road blocks that lie ahead.

INFORMED BUYER'S WILL BECOME STRONGER BUYERS

Before you begin your adventure you need to understand right up front that the information and suggestions provided herein are not intended to be used as the means to get rich quick in the real estate business. Those dreams are most often just schemes and are not a part of

THE REAL ESTATE BUYER'S AWARENESS PLAN.

You will, however, become extremely *aware* of the proven procedures you should follow to locate and purchase the property you desire. You will learn and understand how to recognize some of the problem areas. How to avoid making bad decisions based upon unreliable information or terrible advice that could end up turning into very costly mistakes.

Knowledge is the accumulation of information. Information becomes the buyer's edge.

FINDING AND BUYING THE "RIGHT PROPERTY" IT'S NOT A SCIENCE... IT'S A DEVELOPED ART!!"

Are you intimidated and confused by the home buying process?
Are you a first-time buyer looking for that perfect starter home?
Are you at a time in your life when you must make a big change?
Are you aware of your credit score and if you can make a purchase?
Are you terrified by all those horrible stories you have heard?

I am going to show you how to become better informed and much more knowledgeable of the nuances and fundamentals of real estate.

The purchase of a home or property is definitely a major happening. It does not matter if you are a first-time buyer or someone who has acquired some previous experience, you must go through the entire process each and every time. There are no safe shortcuts. It is in your best interest to become very familiar with the entire searching and buying process before you begin the search.

This **REAL ESTATE BUYER'S AWARENESS PLAN** has been outlined to carefully guide you through the process of finding and buying a property while preparing you for the many challenges that you will certainly encounter. By understanding the basic principles of the real estate business, you will develop the confidence you need to go forward and succeed. Informed buyers are confident buyers.

NOW LET'S GET STARTED!

Step One

Learn the language of real estate and the *Law of Agency.*

The Plain English Language
of Real Estate Terms

In order to feel confident throughout the process of locating and purchasing real estate, you must become familiar with the words and phrases used by most of the professionals in the business.

Don't be intimidated, it's not that difficult!

Real Estate Broker- an individual licensed by the State to represent the public in real estate transactions and who can legally accept payment for those services rendered.

Serious Buyer- that special someone who is ready, willing and able to make a real estate purchase.

Uncle Louie- usually a respected family member who has an opinion on everything and is not reluctant to make it known.

Seller- a person or entity having legal authority to transfer ownership of a property to another person or entity.

Listing Agreement- a contract between a seller and a licensed real estate broker by which the seller appoints the broker as its authorized agent to offer a property for sale to the public.

Co-brokerage- in effect when the commissions earned from the sale of a property is shared among participating brokers.

Buyer's Agent- the real estate broker who has the contract with a buyer to assist in locating a suitable property for purchase and who has agreed to represent the buyer throughout the entire transaction.

Exclusive Buyer's Agent- a buyer's agent working exclusively for the buyer/client, and only the buyer/client, throughout the entire transaction.

Seller's Agent- a real estate broker who has contracted with a seller to list and market a particular property for sale and who represents only the seller throughout the entire transaction.

Agency Disclosure- the customer must be made aware of the agency relationship with the broker before becoming a client.

Open House- an open invitation to the public to inspect a property. It's usually offered by the listing agent. However, in some instances, the invitation will be made by the FSBO seller.

For Sale By Owner (FSBO)- the seller is attempting to market the property without using the services of a licensed real estate professional.

Single Agency- the real estate broker must work for only one client throughout the entire transaction.

Dual Agency- a broker can work for both the seller and the buyer in the same transaction, after a full disclosure is made to all parties.

Designated Agency- (allowed in some states) occurs when the real estate broker appoints and designates a specific agent to represent either the seller or the buyer in the same transaction.

REALTOR®- active member of an association of professionals who is dedicated to the highest standards of conduct in serving the needs of the real estate community and is guided by a strict Code of Ethics.

Multiple Listing Services (MLS)- organizations that distribute listings information to its participating broker members.

Mortgage Broker- a person licensed by the State who acts as an agent for both the lender and the borrower in the same transaction.

Mortgage Loan- has two parts: 1) the note, which is the promise to repay a debt; and 2) the agreement, which is the document that creates the lien with the pledge of real estate as the security.

Adjustable Rate Mortgage (ARM)- whereby the interest rate on the loan amount will be adjusted in accordance with the terms and conditions of the mortgage agreement.

Points- each point is equal to one percent of the loan amount.

Veterans Administration (VA)- the Federal Government agency that guarantees loans issued to qualified veterans.

Federal Housing Administration (FHA)- the Federal Government agency that insures loans issued by approved lenders to qualified borrowers.

Appraisal- the written evaluation, prepared by a recognized licensed entity or individual, for a specific property.

Interest Rate- the charge for borrowing money usually expressed as an annual percentage rate and/or as a percentage of the loan amount.

Commissions- payments to brokers for services rendered, usually based on a percentage of the sales price. Commissions are always negotiable.

Fees- payments to professionals for services rendered, usually a fixed amount which is not based on the sales price.

Escrow- the funds are held in a trust account by a recognized agent, usually to pay taxes and insurance, or may be held as a deposit toward the purchase price of real estate.

Earnest Money- the deposit, made by a potential buyer, offered as evidence of good faith that accompanies a written offer to purchase real estate.

Equity- the value that remains in a property after all the deductions have been made for any current and /or future indebtedness.

Due Diligence- the thorough research of all relevant issues affecting the subject property, performed in a timely manner.

Fico Score (Fair Isaac and Co)- the numerical value, indicating current credit strength, assigned to a credit report.

Attorney Review Period- the time allocated for the review of the terms and conditions of a contract offer to purchase.

Comparative Market Analysis (CMA)- provides very useful information on similar properties in a given area currently on the market, recently removed, under contract, or sold.

Good Faith Estimate- a reliable estimate of the anticipated loan costs and charges due to be paid at closing.

Vicarious Liabilities- the actions or statements made by an agent that could become the responsibility of the client.

Pre-qualification- determines the Buyer's purchasing power.

Pre-approved- the confirmation by a lender of the mortgage loan amount available to a borrower on a specific loan application.

Adult Communities- housing units established and designed for a specific adult lifestyle.

Condominium Ownership- a multi-unit complex in which the apartments are individually owned, however, the common areas exist as a shared ownership.

Agency Relationships

Single Agency- in effect, when the real estate agent works for only one client in the transaction, the seller or the buyer, but not for both.

Dual Agency- in effect when the broker works for both the seller and the buyer, in the same transaction. Be aware that the broker must fully disclose this fact to each party and receive the informed written consent from both parties.

The Dual Agency Broker accepts the risk and the responsibility of walking a very fine line when attempting to "fairly and honestly" represent both parties in the same transaction. This comment is by no means a veiled attempt to suggest it can't happen. It can, it has, and it most likely will continue to happen.

In most cases the transactions were completed successfully and all parties are still very satisfied with the outcome. However, there have been some situations that did not turn out as expected. One or both of the participants feel as if they have been taken advantage of and the law suits start. In those cases no one wins. That is not entirely accurate. Let's say, the lawyers win.

In the event you are Internet literate, look up the information available on the Law of Agency. Become better informed before you become a victim.

Designated Agency- occurs when a broker takes a listing and appoints the listing agent as the designated agent of the seller and excludes all other agents in the office from that relationship. When an agent works with a buyer on that listing, the broker appoints the agent as the designated agent of the buyer for the transaction and excludes all other agents from that relationship. This form of agency is not recognized or permitted in all states. Be sure to check the laws in your particular state.

Non-agency Relationships- practiced in some states, when licensees work with buyers and sellers in a non-agency capacity. In this circumstance, the agent acts in a neutral position for both parties in a given transaction. Non-agency relationships vary from state to state. The broker is required to disclose the relationship in a timely fashion.

The National Association of Realtors (NAR)- whose members are known as REALTORS. It is one of the largest trade associations in North America representing over 1.2 million members who are involved in the many aspects of the residential and commercial real estate industries. The (NAR) also functions as a self-regulatory organization for the real estate brokerage business. The organization is headquartered in Chicago. Take the time to learn more and get familiar with this organization by looking at their site: www.REALTOR.org.

Real Estate Buyer's Agent Council (REBAC)- a subsidiary of (NAR).

(REBAC) is the world's largest organization of real estate professionals. With a focus on *buyer representation* and by promoting specialized training and ongoing skill development,

REBAC helps its members, and the home buyers who work with them, to experience more successful real estate transactions.

I urge you to research REBAC at www.REBAC.net. You will recognize the importance of a Buyer's Representative and better understand the benefits and protections you receive when working with an Exclusive Buyer's Agent.

INFORMED BUYER'S

ARE

BETTER BUYERS

REALTOR®

The Realtors Code of Ethics and Standards of Practice, establishes certain obligations that may be higher than those mandated by law. In any instance where the Realtors Code of Ethics is more restrictive than the real estate laws, Realtors *must* comply with the standards set out by the NAR Code of Ethics. Realtors are devoted to maintain these standards and will always conduct themselves accordingly. Realtors pledge to protect and promote the interests of their clients. Visit the website at www.PCBOR.com.

CHOOSE A REALTOR

USE A REALTOR

Do you know who is on your side and looking out for you?

It's A Jungle Out There

The old doctrine of *"caveat emptor"* which used to have the meaning, "LET THE BUYER BEWARE", is outdated and no longer has a place in this modern day real estate market.

Now-a-day's, the sophisticated *BUYER IS AWARE*—and usually well informed of the issues that affect a real estate purchase. Being *aware* of all the facts and conditions of a property long before the purchase is the buyer's best protection from horrible results. Knowledge is the only safe defense against prejudicial information or just plain terrible advice.

AWARENESS*THE BUYER'S EDGE*ADVANTAGE BUYER

The Casual Shopper

In the real estate marketplace, there exists a certain group of people whom I shall label the casual shopper. These people have accepted almost all of the open house invitations, have visited a large number of homes, are familiar with many of the available properties, and actually enjoy the experience, but they will never ever become buyers. They are always "just looking". The activity is similar to the "window shopper" at the mall.

There are some who are only curious. They want to know more about the house down the street that's for sale. How much are they asking for it? What condition is it in? Is it larger or smaller than theirs? If they decide they want to sell theirs, can they get the same price, or maybe a little more?

There are others who will look at areas in which the homes are way out of their price range. They select a local agent, one who doesn't know them yet, to set up appointments to visit a few homes. Most agents will spend a lot of time working with this "potential buyer" until they realize this "customer" will never become a serious buyer. They are also "just looking."

This casual shopper unjustly takes up a lot of valuable time from these very accommodating real estate agents and reduces the time these professionals have available to service and assist the serious buyer. This conduct, by this shopper, is inconsiderate and just not right. But it does continue to happen.

For this casual shopper the following friendly advice is offered.

Go forth into that "casual shoppers" paradise of real estate and spend all your leisure time driving through different neighborhoods looking at properties you shall never buy, because

> you just don't like the area;

> the house is too large or just a little too small;

> the asking price is absolutely outrageous;

> you would never buy it ... just because

However, leave the rest of us alone to concentrate on assisting the serious buyer through the exciting challenge of locating and purchasing that "just right property."

The Serious Buyer (SB)

In a real estate transaction, the serious buyer (SB) is that special someone who has made the decision to locate and purchase a home or property and is prepared to make a sincere commitment to pursue and accomplish that goal. They understand the challenges, realize the effort needed and are ready to go.

This (SB) may have started out as the casual shopper, more curious of the current housing market than actually interested in making a very serious commitment to actively locate and purchase a property.

However, sometimes something kicks in. Perhaps a certain property catches their attention and gets the juices flowing. Or maybe a change occurs in their lifestyle that has an effect on their housing needs.

In any event, they become curious or motivated enough to begin looking at a few properties. Their adventure is underway. Now is the time when this (SB) should start to follow the searching process described in this Buyer's Guide.

This *Real Estate Buyer's Awareness Plan* is directed to that person.

When the (SB) makes the decision to engage the services of a real estate professional, a Buyer's Agent, the (SB) becomes the client. Instantly the (SB) is now the most important party in the transaction. The (SB) takes full control of all present and future real estate decisions.

*NO BUYER*NO SALE*

That's it and, because buyers are that important, they should be the most knowledgeable people in the transaction. The fact is too many *buyers* are not adequately informed, nor do they spend enough time or effort to learn and understand all the facts about a property before they commit to buy the property. Even though this is probably the largest single purchase they will ever make, they go about the process in a very casual manner.

A CASUAL EFFORT WILL NOT PRODUCE GOOD RESULTS!

YOU NEED AN ORGANIZED PLAN TO REACH YOUR GOAL!

Okay, Let's Go Shopping

The process of shopping for a home or property to purchase can be a pleasant adventure or a terrifying experience. A disciplined effort, along with the dedication of a lot of time can be the controlling factors to the final outcome.

The actual ownership of a home or property may be the happy reward for the time and effort well spent, or it can be an *albatross,* the result of poor decisions that were made based upon limited information or bad advice. Don't accept whatever you are told as a fact. Find out for yourself. Do the research. It's called DUE DILIGENCE.

Many potential *buyers* begin this adventure by reading through the real estate section of the newspapers and home sales magazines. They may also drive through random areas looking for properties with "for sale" signs and "open house" invitations displayed.

When a certain property seems to have some potential, they try to make contact directly with a seller or through the listing real estate agent to arrange for a closer inspection of the property.

Computer savvy buyers may attempt to find the right property using the Internet as their source for information. Although this method has some value, it is also limited. Only on very rare occasions will these methods prove to be successful.

More often than not, these procedures will be frustrating experiences and a constant source of aggravation, because appointments will be canceled without prior notice, the properties are not suitable to their needs, or the asking price is absolutely outrageous. These are only a few reasons.

Yes! You Can Try to Go It Alone

If (1) you are mentally and emotionally prepared, (2) you have a great deal of time available, (3) you are excited and full of energy, (4) you have finished reading through this buyer's guide, and (5) you have understood all or most of the information presented, perhaps then you can try to go for it on your own. But, before you try, you must develop an acute sense of awareness.

However, you have an option. This may be the right time to introduce you to the exclusive buyer's agent concept.

The Exclusive Buyer's Agent (EBA)

With the assistance of an (EBA), who works exclusively for you and only you, the buyer, and represents only you throughout the entire transaction, you will become better informed to make the right buying decisions.

Your (EBA) "does all the walking" for you!

Your (EBA) has the ways and means to locate those properties that seem to meet your requirements. Your (EBA) will research and identify all those that appear to qualify.

When a property comes close to matching your profile your (EBA) will make a preliminary visit to assess the potential fit. You thereby save a great deal of valuable time and avoid the wasted effort usually spent chasing the "wrong properties," those that just don't make it.

With your permission, arrangements will then be made for you to make your personal house inspection. You should take advantage of each opportunity. The greater number of houses you get to see, the more aware you will become of the opportunities available to you.

After you have completed your personal inspection, your buyer's agent will follow up on those homes that piqued your interest and respond to any and all concerns that you may raise. Such as the composition of the neighborhood and the quality of the school system, along with many other matters that may affect your decision to purchase.

Are you a Customer or a Client?

Are you *aware* of the critical difference between a customer and a client? Let me describe the important distinction between the two words.

A *customer* is someone who has expressed some casual interest in obtaining information on one or perhaps more than one property. A real estate agent will most certainly work *with* this customer and try to provide some useful service. However there is no agency relationship between the parties. This agent is simply working *with* the customer. Absolutely no fiduciary exists.

Nevertheless, real estate agents still have a responsibility to treat any and all customers fairly, honestly, and without any misrepresentations. They should provide customers with a standard of professionalism that is reasonable and expected in the industry. They must not make any statements that could be considered fraudulent or misleading.

A *client,* on the other hand, is someone with whom an agency relationship has been established. This relationship is legally binding and is a very critical part of the entire transaction. In this situation the real estate agents have a fiduciary obligation to their client and must place the interests of that client ahead of all others, including their own.

This professional real estate agent is now working *for* the client.

Fiduciary

A fiduciary occurs when an agent accepts the authorization of a client to act on behalf of that client in a specific real estate transaction. As a fiduciary this buyer's agent is now in a position of trust and owes loyalty to the client.

All real estate agents must adhere to the (NAR) National Association of Realtors Code of Ethics whenever dealing with either customers or clients. This Code of Ethics specifically outlines the obligations realtors have to the public and their clients in all real estate transactions.

A buyer's agent must disclose all material facts and information about the property to the client. For example, the agent may have learned something crucial about the seller's motivation or financial situation. The client can then use this knowledge to make an informed decision.

However, this buyer's agent must never ever divulge any of the client's confidential information to anyone, especially the seller or the seller's agent.

Loyalty to a client is of upmost importance. Never under any circumstances should the buyer's agent disclose any matters of financing, the motivation to purchase, or any other facts that could restrict a client's negotiating position.

In addition, the Law of Agency applies. This agency relationship has specific duties all agents must perform. Ask your agent for a copy of the Code of Ethics and be sure to read it. You must become familiar with and *aware* of the duties and responsibilities of your agent if you expect to be treated fairly.

In any real estate transaction money and of course motivation are usually the most important issues to both the sellers and the buyers.

Seller's Representation

Most buyers assume (*ass-u-n-me*) that they are being represented by that seller's real estate agent they happened to meet when they looked at that house they did not like but who since then has been spending a lot of time with them showing them other great properties all over town.

Not So, Grasshopper

This pleasant, seemingly helpful seller's agent is working *for the seller* of those properties. Yes, that's correct, even those properties that are listed with other brokers. *Be aware, you are a customer not a client.*

This agent has a fiduciary responsibility to all those sellers through the Law of Agency and should have disclosed this important fact to you, the potential buyer, immediately at first contact.

Therefore, when visiting a property with this seller's agent, you must control your emotions. No *oohs* and *aahs* are permitted. Do not express any signs of enthusiasm or eagerness to purchase when you are in the presence of the seller or the seller's agent. These are a definite no-no! Believe me! Just don't do it!

In addition, be especially *aware* that these sellers' agents have a duty, an obligation, and a responsibility to divulge any and all information to the seller/client that they may have learned about you. You are the potential buyer and they would like to know as much as possible about you and your particular situation.

For example, they can disclose personal circumstances that may have an impact on your motivation to purchase, or perhaps how high in price you would go even though you may be offering less than that amount the first time around. Also, anything and everything else that you assumed was just general conversation but in fact were very personal informational facts these sellers' agents can use to the benefit of their client.

The seller's agent is paid a commission for selling these properties. They are responsible to the seller for getting the highest price possible. The sales agent's commission is usually based upon a percentage of the final sales price. Let me assure you, they are not bad people and It's not personal; it's just business!

The higher the sales price the better.

Buyer's Representation

Enter the exclusive buyer's agent, who works *for the buyer only* and will negotiate solely on behalf of the buyer for the lowest possible price with the best terms and conditions. *The lower the purchase price the better.*

When the payment to the buyer's agent is a "fixed-fee" amount, that has been pre-determined between the parties and not based upon the final purchase price, the lowest possible purchase price has no impact on the fee earned by the buyer's agent. That's what "fixed fee" means.

Over time the industry has established certain fee and commission standards. *Be aware* however, that all fees and commissions are fully negotiable between the clients and their real estate brokers.

In most cases the listing agreement will stipulate the portion of the sales commission the listing broker will co-broke with a buyer's agent.

Depending upon the terms and conditions of the fees to be paid by you to your buyer's agent, in your exclusive buyer's agreement, the monies received by your buyer's agent, in this co-broke situation, are usually applied to the fixed fee amount. As the process moves along, having someone on your side is beneficial.

Buyer's representation does not cost; it pays!

The Buyer Provides All the Money

The most common misunderstanding and objection to the buyer's agent concept, is the fee the buyers must pay to their agent. Some buyers really believe that the fees and commissions paid to the real estate brokers must be coming from the seller's money. Although that thought appears to be the case, it is not a completely accurate assumption.

Follow me on this. Let me break it down.

The seller will agree to accept a purchase price offer only after a complete accounting of the costs and charges has been made. This includes all the payments for all the fees and commissions. Yes, even the commissions that are to be paid to both the buyer's and the seller's agents. The seller is mostly interested in the net result. That is the bottom line.

Sophisticated buyers understand this reality and realize that the monies being made available in the real estate transaction are being provided through the funds of the buyer. Take a few moments to think about it.

No Buyer**No Money**No Sale

No Commissions**No Fees

Step Three

Organize a viable plan before you begin the searching phase.

The Buyer's Awareness Plan

Whether you have decided to go for it alone or you have chosen a buyer's agent, you must organize a detailed plan before you eagerly venture out into the world of the unknown. In order to properly construct an effective plan for finding and buying the "right property," you must explore each of the various parts that make up the entire experience. You start with the search and continue through to closing.

Be as honest and forthright as possible in your analysis of each of the different factors that will affect your decision making. Do not hurry through this exercise. Your attention to details at this stage of the process will make the rest of the adventure a much more enjoyable experience. Home ownership is a serious commitment and should be approached from that perspective.

Motivation is the incentive to find, buy, and own real estate.

A person assumes many duties, responsibilities and obligations upon becoming a property owner, and not everyone is suited to owning a home. The time, effort, cost, and risk of home ownership must be considered. Are you ready for the challenge? Are you sure?

The maintenance of a home or property is simple and easy when you are a tenant. Not if, but when, a problem occurs you simply call the landlord. You explain the situation and you wait for a response. If you don't get one, you call again! Sooner or later it's done. Problem solved.

However, when you become the owner, there is no one to call. You are now the one responsible for the repairs and associated costs. Are you confident that you are ready to handle this new assignment?

Some people have the ability to work with tools and actually enjoy the time and effort needed to take on the maintenance and repair projects. They always seem to have another project lined up. And, they take a lot of pride in their workmanship when the job is finished.

Then, of course, there are others who will not or cannot get involved in these matters. In that case, they need to be financially capable of paying all the costs, as they come up. And, these costs do come up.

The Financial Risks and Rewards

Potential buyers also need to be *aware* of certain financial risks that are always present. Real estate has always been a good solid long-term investment. And although the value of most properties will probably increase over time, there are no guarantees.

You should begin the financial analysis by comparing your current monthly costs for your rent payments against the projected costs of paying the principal, interest, taxes and insurance (PITI). For assistance in this area, refer to the buyer's borrowing capacity section in *Step Six* to arrive at your probable monthly (PITI) payment amount.

Keep in mind that your landlord has control over the rental amount, which can increase as the landlord sees fit. In most cases, the amount needed for your mortgage payment can be structured in such a way so it will remain constant for the entire term of the mortgage.

Other money and motivational issues to ponder should be your short-term and long-term plans. How long do you think you may be living in your present location? Could your housing requirements be affected by a change to your employment opportunities?

Perhaps there is a change coming in the makeup of your lifestyle, like getting married or planning a family. Is your present family growing?

Short-term is usually less than two years. If this is your situation, then renting is probably the most sensible decision at the present time. You could be confronted with financial loss if you purchased a property and suddenly, within the two-year period and under duress, you must place the property on the market. You should give some serious thought to this aspect while you are in the process of making the final decision.

Should you have a longer-term plan, you most likely will benefit from homeownership. While living in your own home you certainly will have accumulated some equity as you made your mortgage payments and reduced the balance of the mortgage loan. The payments are almost like a forced savings plan that becomes a part of your regular budget.

If, or when, you decide that it's time to sell, you should be in a stronger financial position. Let me be very clear—there are no guarantees!

There is always a risk attached to owning real estate.

Execute the Plan

By this time you should have developed a strong and secure attitude to reinforce the fact that you are the buyer. Therefore, you are in control of every situation and will not be intimidated by anyone on any issue.

Should you find yourself uninformed on any specific issue or subject at any particular time, you have the confidence and presence of mind to know how, when, and where to seek capable professional guidance.

You must be prepared to:

Allocate a realistic portion of time to accomplish the task. The average time to find a desirable property is ten weeks and the average time to process a mortgage is eight weeks.

Investigate the condition of each property and know where to look for defects; learn how to recognize the potential problems and determine the cost and effect of a solution.

Analyze the information that is being provided and be able to validate the accuracy or identify the errors.

Spend the time to research the communities of interest.

Engage the services of qualified professionals.

Negotiate for the lowest price and best terms because you can sense the seller's motivation to sell and anticipate the urgency to accept a reasonable offer

Arrange for financing. Earmark the cash needed to make the purchase.

Calculate your purchasing power and submit a loan application.

Determine the present market value of the property by making comparisons to similar properties.

First-Time Buyers (FTB)

What is your motivation? Do you have financing? How about attitude?

If you fit into this group of potential buyers, you may have begun to recognize the economic advantages of owning a home and building equity instead of always paying rent. Rather than getting a rent receipt each month, you can start to accumulate equity. It is a great concept.

Right now is the best time in a very long time for the (FTB) to take advantage of the slump in the housing market. Mortgage rates are at an all time low. The drop in home prices to a more realistic level has made some great opportunities available.

For the (FTB) who may be considering the purchase of a home in the foreseeable future you should start the mortgage process ASAP. It's never too early to get yourself pre-qualified for a mortgage loan. In the event you happen to find a home of your choice, you will be in a good position to make the move quickly. When you least expect it bam bam! That is how fast great deals can happen. That low offer you made, that you thought was dead, just got accepted. And you are ready to go!

Some first-time buyers (FTB) have legitimate reservations regarding the ownership of a home versus renting. In most situations, the major concern in making the final decision, is the financial aspect. Analyze your particular situation. Does it make better sense to rent or to own?

There may be certain tax benefits that could be available. Obviously there are also some serious liabilities and obligations. As soon as possible, you should consult your tax advisor and your attorney for advice. They can assist you in evaluating your financial position.

In addition to the financial aspect, home ownership can provide some people with the satisfaction and security of knowing where they will be residing for the foreseeable future. It is a very comfortable feeling.

For most people, having roots in a neighborhood, along with the pride of home ownership, can be a very important motivator for making the final decision to find, buy and own the "right property."

Do You Have the Cash?

Usually a down payment of 10 percent to 20 percent is required in order to obtain a conventional mortgage loan. However, there are many different mortgage plans available. Consult a mortgage broker.

Do you know your credit score? Do you have any idea of how much you can afford to pay for your home? What is the maximum you want to spend for your home? These questions and more must be answered before you begin the search.

Some FTBs do not have the advantage of established credit and to get approved for a conventional loan can be impossible. The mortgage process can take a few weeks or longer for first time buyers.

For the FTB who qualifies, a VA or FHA loan program may be the way to go. Contact the VA or FHA office to learn more. Use the web.

My First House

I purchased my first home in 1957 for $12,700.00. Yes, you can believe it. They were the good old days. The house was one of those 1950s tract houses. It was approximately 1300 square feet. It had the usual 3 bedrooms and 1 bathroom. Although it was a little on the small side, by today's standards, it was all I needed and could afford at the time.

However, being in the building business, I was able to add a garage on to the house and turned the cellar into a finished basement.

After a few years, as our family size changed, we sold that house and moved to a larger home in the same general area. Of course we made a small profit that we applied to the purchase our new home.

Today, because of inflation and many other economic reasons, that house has a market value of around $275,000.00. Although this appears to be a fantastic situation that everyone should try, you must be *aware* there are no guarantees of future results.

Later, as our lifestyle changed, we bought and sold a few more houses. I will admit that not all those moves worked out as well as the first one.

We were learning as we went along. Not a good way to go and certainly not recommended in today's climate. Get informed and become *aware*. Informed buyers are stronger buyers.

Seasoned Owners

There are other serious buyers who are currently homeowners and may be experiencing a major change in their present lifestyle. They could be faced with the need for more space for a growing family or perhaps a little less space because they have become "empty nesters." Their kids have grown and have moved out of the house. It's time to downsize.

For the potential buyer in this situation, the sale of an existing home is usually necessary in order to make a purchase of another property. This dilemma can create the classic "chicken and egg" syndrome, whereby one event is predicated on the other. At this point, which event must happen first, the sale or the purchase?

I suggest that both actions need to happen concurrently. Review your financial circumstances and determine the amount of money you are willing to apply to another purchase before you begin house-hunting.

Have a realtor prepare a CMA that will suggest a value for your present home. Depending on where you intend to relocate you can get a CMA from a realtor in that location to get a feeling of local values.

Now you can set the asking price for your present home while you go shopping for properties within your established price range.

Of course, setting the right asking price for the sale of the existing home would probably encourage a quick sale and therefore expedite the purchase of a different property.

These seasoned owners are probably familiar with the nuances of the buying and selling process. Most likely they have started to take the same basic steps required of anyone looking to find and purchase a property. They will get all the ducks lined up well in advance.

There are no acceptable shortcuts!

A Buyer's Market

Timing is always very important in almost any activity. Although it is still a "buyer's market," because the interest rates for mortgage loans are at the lowest in a very long time, be *sensitive* and watch the housing market trends. Mortgage rates and terms are constantly changing.

Real estate prices have dropped to a more realistic level. The supply of properties is rather substantial. However, as the inventory is bought up and fewer properties remain available, buying opportunities will most definitely change. The change may happen very quickly.

Timing is always a crapshoot. You do need a little-bit-of-luck. Right now there are properties on the market that are reasonably priced and have good potential investment value. Those are the properties you would like to find. They are out there, but you must be *alert* and know how and where to search for them. Have your (EBA) assist you.

If you are on your own, you must put in the time and effort to find the right deal, the one that is best for your situation. Above all, don't get discouraged. The search time could be as long as a few months. Even then there are no guarantees you will find the right one for you.

Use the Internet as a reliable source of information. There are many sites that provide local listings. You can view them on your computer at your own pace. The technology is out there. Take advantage of it.

If, however, you have elected to engage the services of a buyer's agent, your agent should be doing all the leg work for you. Keep in touch on a regular basis. If you are not getting the service you expected you must speak up. You should make your feelings known immediately.

Just another reminder: *you are the buyer*!

A Seller's Market

A few years ago the value some homeowners placed on their properties reached an all-time high. Most real estate agents were very *aware* of the buying frenzy and took advantage of the opportunity. They encouraged sellers to set high asking prices. You can almost hear them say "don't worry, just give us the listing, we can get you the highest price". And, in most cases, they did. This was a seller's market of the worst kind.

For most buyers, mortgages were readily available to almost anyone who wanted one. The buying boom was on and the prices of homes reflected the demand. Some sellers were getting multiple offers.

You may have heard the stories that in certain areas there were bidding wars for the same property. At the time, it may have been hard for you to believe, but it was absolutely true.

Many homes were sold just as quickly as they were listed. The asking prices just kept on going higher and higher, with no end in sight. This was probably the start of the collapse of the real estate market.

Some sellers, along with their real estate agents made a lot of money. As expected, some buyers took a serious financial hit. Mortgage lenders also got burned although mortgage brokers made out very well.

Many people purchased homes they really could not afford to own. In some cases, these homeowners are now facing serious consequences. You are probably well *aware* of the number of foreclosures and homes that are "underwater." This entire mess could have been avoided.

Be Realistic

Evaluate and then reevaluate your motivation for taking this big step. Motivation and timing could become the most important factors in making the final decision.

Pay attention to the marketplace. Do not become a negative statistic.

The process for finding and buying the "right property" could take a while. On average it's about six months from start to finish.

When you are positively ready ... go for it!

Step Four

Are you familiar with the three famous words of wisdom?

Location... Location ... Location

Now interchange the words with ...Urban ... Suburban ... Rural..

Each has an obvious meaning and describes a specific environment.

Your nearest neighbor could be three feet away across the alley, or three miles down the road. Adequate attention should be given to the location aspect, which is always a very personal choice. Almost everything you do and everyone with whom you do it will be affected by the location selected. Do not rush through this deliberation. Take your time, it's too important.

Consider the probability of finding your "right property" in any given area. Are the types and prices of your desired property available in this location?

Will you be wasting your time with a futile search? What are the chances of finding a "farm" in center city? Although possible, not very realistic!

Why This Particular Location?

The short list may include the travel time to your present or near future employment opportunities. Or perhaps access to religious and educational institutions. Consider the distances to shopping and recreational facilities, the availability of public or private transportation, or any other interests you may have. Check your priority list. You do have one don't you? If not, go to *Step Seven* for suggestions. Write up your list and refer to it often!

Be Sure to Stay Focused

Once you have made the selection of a general area, you must then zero in on specific neighborhoods. Make a thorough inspection by driving around in the daytime and also in the evening. Stop in at the local stores, post office, restaurants, or gasoline station and speak with the people there. Get a feel for the personality of the residents. Take the time to become *aware* and keep in mind that these people may soon be your new neighbors.

In my neighborhood, I know the people living next to me on either side, in the back and across the street. I believe it's important to know them. Most of us are *alert* to strangers visiting in the area. We have a neighborhood watch.

The composite of the neighborhood should be a priority concern. Is it made up of families with younger children? Or is it a more adult community with retired people? The answers may have an effect on your final decision.

Ask the people living in the area about public services, such as police, fire, and emergency units. Stop in at the police station and ask about reported vandalism and burglaries.

Do you have school-age children that need public transportation? Can they walk to school? How far away is the ball field, the library, or the recreation center? Visit the school administration office. Inquire about the after-school programs. Talk about lunch programs and any other school activities.

Visit some websites that can provide information on area schools. There are plenty of sites available. Here are two to get you started:

www.greatschools.org   www.schoolmatters.com

Do not be embarrassed to ask anyone any questions on any of the issues about which you have a concern. Do you feel safe and secure? Are you comfortable? You must become *aware* before you purchase, not after you have moved in. By then it's too late.

Ask questions! Get answers!

Here are some other websites you can look into to get good information: www.neighborhoodscout.com www.familywatchdog.us

When you are familiar with an area, you may not need to spend a lot of time with certain details; however, do not move quickly through this phase as you may be living at this location for quite a while.

Would you enjoy being a gentlemen farmer? If so, there are many properties out there that may accommodate your interests. Usually ten acres or more will satisfy the "farm" requirements. There may be tax credits available for growing certain crops or raising farm animals. It's possible to make a few dollars while enjoying being a "farmer."

A long time ago, when my kids were growing up, I rented a farm where we kept a few horses. It was a fantastic experience. Try it you may like it. I did! We had a great time and still enjoy the memories.

Be Alert

What is the chance of a major change occurring that could have an impact on future value? Find out if any plans exist to alter the road systems or a proposal to construct a major industrial park or a trash-recycling station.

In certain locations property values may have dropped because of a not in my backyard (NIMBY) facility being built. Had the buyer gone through a detailed *due-diligence* effort prior to making the purchase, the problem could have been avoided. A buyer would have been *aware* of the change in zoning being planned for the adjoining vacant land *before* buying the house. Back then it looked like a nice place for a park.

In other cases, the cause was due to unforeseen issues over which the property owner had no control. For example, a large employer could have moved out of the area. Suddenly people are losing their homes to foreclosure and are moving out to find employment. In the wake of this situation a lot of homes instantly hit the market. Values drop.

Foreclosures

Regrettably, some people find themselves in financial difficulties and have lost their property to a foreclosure proceeding. In many cases the problem was not caused by them. It is an unfortunate situation, but it is reality.

In some locations of the country, or in a particular area of any state, a large number of foreclosures seem to be more prevalent. Although this condition is not good for those with the problem, it may be an opportunity for some people to find and make a great deal. You can find these homes on the web.

If you are working with a buyer's agent, you will have reliable information upon which you can make an informed decision. Your buyer's agent will have access to the foreclosed properties and can offer some insight relevant to the issue, while keeping your best interest as the main focus.

If the foreclosure proceedings have been completed, the lender has already taken possession. And, if the property has been on the market for quite a while, the lender/current owner is usually interested in a quick sale.

The asking price is probably on the lower side of true value. Depending on your financial situation, you could be in a position to move forward quickly.

However, before you instantly jump into what appears to be a great deal, you must consider the probability that the property values in the area could continue to decline. You must have the mind-set and the financial stability to ride out the current market conditions. It could take a while for the values to creep back up. It really is a little risky.

Short Sales

Short sales are quite different from foreclosures. In a short sale, the lender and the home owner have agreed to attempt to sell the property prior to a foreclosure. Short sales are a complicated type of transaction and usually have a very high failure rate. In some cases the property was foreclosed before the short sale transaction could be completed.

If you get involved in one of these purchases, be sure to have an expert on your side. Engage the services of a Realtor who specializes in short sales.

Step Five

You should develop an advanced level of *Awareness.*

Awareness... and how it applies to buying real estate

In the dictionary, the synonyms of awareness include the following:

Aware—denotes knowledge of something through information.

Sensitive—implies knowledge gained by sensing/perceiving.

Alert—stresses knowledge with the capacity of a swift response.

Vigilant—infers perception of what is potentially dangerous.

Each of these words carries a significant meaning. When you begin to understand them you will develop the attitude needed to assure success in your house hunting and buying adventure

The point here is to emphasize the meaning and importance of your *awareness* of each detail that could possibly affect the use or value of the home or property you are considering for purchase.

Develop Your Level of Awareness

Do not forget, you are the buyer. You have the right to ask questions about everything from everyone, especially from the seller—that's if the seller's sales agent will let you get close enough to ask. Usually the sales agent will keep the seller away from the buyer. In that event, the selling agent should be asked to provide the answers to all your questions.

Become *aware* of the land. The parts you can see and those you can't. Obtain a copy of the latest survey. It will show the size, shape, easements, rights of way, encroachments, improvements, etc. Be satisfied that there are no issues or potential problems about which you have any concerns.

Pay attention to the condition of the landscaping, lawns, shrubs, and trees. Do they appear to be healthy and growing or are they decaying?

Take a close look at the larger older trees. Are the roots lifting the public sidewalks? A situation like that could become a violation of the building code. Address the matter now. If necessary, contact the local code official. Ask the right questions; get the complete answers.

Inspect the driveways, sidewalks, steps, walls, and patios, etc., for cracks and signs of settlement or the need for repairs. These are some of the issues that determine value and of course the amount of your offer to purchase.

Be present at the site during a rainstorm so you can observe the condition of the drainage systems and water run off. Do you see any signs of standing or stagnant water? A problem like this could be a future Health Department violation. You must try to avoid these types of problems.

Ask questions about utilities and service lines such as water, gas, sewer, telephone, TV cable, wells, septic systems, drainage, etc. Where are they located, and are they all in reasonably good working order?

Also, another very important issue to you is the existence of an oil tank. If a tank is presently being used, you need to become *aware* of the condition. How old is it? How large is it? Perhaps a tank has been abandoned but not removed. There may be potential liability for clean-up costs in the event of an old oil spill. This is reality.

Walk all around the property. Go along the perimeters of the property and take a good look at the condition of the adjoining properties. Are they well maintained or are they run down? Could there be an adverse impact on future value? If possible, try to meet the residents.

In most states, the seller must disclose all material facts known about the property to a potential buyer. Should the buyer decide to continue forward with the purchase of the property and has the complete and full knowledge of the potential problems, the seller will most likely be held harmless and relieved of all future liabilities.

Some buyers will take for granted that the information provided them is complete and accurate in every detail. However, in the real world that is not always the case. As indicated by the many lawsuits filed, buyers will sue sellers and everyone else should they find a problem after the transaction has been completed.

By that time, the damage has been done and there is nothing left but lawsuits, endless litigations, and a lot of expenses.

Awareness of the Condition of the House

Awareness that in certain situations, problems with the land or the buildings can be more costly to resolve or correct than you are willing to accept.

Components That Are Visible

The general overall appearance of the exterior, also known as the curb appeal, is usually an indication of the pride of ownership being expressed by the homeowner. The condition of the exterior is often a good indicator of what you can expect to find on the inside. Your level of awareness and certainly your first impressions are extremely important at this early stage.

Be *alert* to the warning signs of poor maintenance or lack of repairs. Look for that freshly painted wall or roof overhang, which may be hiding a water leak or a crack in the structure. Investigate for loose or rusted railings, peeling paint, broken glass, missing gutters or downspouts and any other openly visible things.

However, be *aware* that most sellers do some cosmetic work and sprucing up just before they offer the property for sale. This is a common practice and it should be expected.

Once inside the building, you should make a thorough but brief walkthrough of the arrangement of all the rooms. Take note of the traffic flow and the layout of all the rooms. Do you find yourself disoriented or very comfortable? Could you see yourself living here?

Be *sensitive* and get a feeling for the shapes and sizes of the spaces to determine if there is any potential for your use. In the event you find anything you do not like, get out of there as quickly as possible. Trust your first instincts. They are usually right.

Don't subject yourself to a sales pitch from the sales agent or from anyone else. Do not spend any more of your time than necessary. You are not obligated to explain your actions or feelings to anyone. Keep in mind that you are the potential buyer. You are in control!

However, in the event you are comfortable with what you see to this point and would like to make a more thorough inspection, you should take as much time as you feel you need to be sure this house might be the "right one" for you.

All interested parties, *yes, including your Uncle Louie,* should take the walkthrough together so that everyone will have the opportunity to compare notes at the same time. An open and forthright discussion should take place. It's important to express your feelings.

Take some measurements of the important spaces to be sure that your intended use can be accommodated. Will your furniture fit in the areas you have in mind, or must you make concessions? Review your priority list. You do have one, don't you? If not, make one!

Walk through every room and look into all the spaces. Open every door you see, no matter if it's a closet or a storage area. Be sure to stay *alert* and be *vigilant.* Look for the signs of water leaks and mold, especially on the ceilings and walls under bathrooms and kitchens. Also look under the cabinets and the dark spaces of the basement.

Open every faucet and flush every toilet bowl. This action may reveal the first signs of potential plumbing problems. Check the condition of the bathtub. This is a very important issue because of the amount of work and the cost involved to remove and replace the fixture. Sure the tub can be resurfaced, but that work is not free. It can cost a lot of money. This may become an item to negotiate.

If you are expecting to use the existing kitchen appliances or hot water heater, you will want to be certain that these units are in good working order. Turn all the dials on the stove and check inside the oven. Run the dishwasher, the disposal unit, and any other electrical appliances while you pay attention to notice any overloads to the electrical systems. Ask about the size of the electrical service.

Be sure to make notes of whatever you see so you can refresh your memory at some later date. If possible, take as many pictures as you can of those areas of concern. You will be visiting more than one property and it is not always easy to keep all the facts in the proper order. Stay focused.

The Parts You Cannot See

Latent defects that may be known to the seller or the sales agent but are not easily discernable to the potential buyer through an ordinary inspection routine must be addressed.

For instance, the new homeowner may be required, by local code, to upgrade the electrical system and perhaps increase the size of the electrical service coming into the building. This could be expensive.

In many states, the seller is required by law to provide the potential buyer with a completed disclosure form. If the property is listed with an agent, the disclosure form will be available for your review. In the case of a property being marketed by a FSBO, you must ask for a copy of the completed form.

Ask questions and be sure to get complete answers from the seller about the mechanical and electrical systems. It's not unreasonable to expect a seller or a sales agent to disclose any known defects to a buyer and avoid any future legal actions.

In some cases you may find that the seller has purchased a home inspection report and is willing to make a copy of that report available to you. You may also be permitted to speak with that inspector to get a feeling for the conditions of the property. It is becoming a common occurrence. Most sophisticated sellers and sales agents know the importance and understand the benefits of full disclosure to the potential buyer.

You or your buyer's agent realtor must obtain information from the seller regarding the known existence of any lead-based paint that may be present in the house. In the event a home inspection report is not available, the seller must provide you with the opportunity to make a lead-based paint inspection.

Although the lead-based paint issue is mostly of concern in those "older homes," built before 1978, nonetheless you need to know for sure. Some towns may require a written statement from a certified home inspection service, prior to the issuance of a new certificate of occupancy.

Professional Home Inspector

If in fact you feel you have found the "right property," it is now the time to engage the services of your own inspector. At this point, if you are being told that you don't need to waste the money to hire a professional inspector, don't listen! Hire one anyway. ASAP.

Do your own research. Perhaps you know someone who has used this type of service and has a recommendation. Be sure that the one you hire is properly licensed and fully insured. Get verifications.

Yes, I know it's true that everyone has a good friend or a close relative like your *Uncle Louie* who is the self-proclaimed expert on everything. However, you should choose a professional and not lose a friend—yes, especially your *Uncle Louie!*

You must not expect your real estate professional to provide any sort of advice or expertise in this area. Most agents are not qualified, and even if they have some experience, they should not offer any opinions. Do not buy a property *as is* without a home inspection report. You will be at risk and most likely you will regret it!

Be aware of the conditions before you buy.

Many of the mortgage-lending institutions are demanding a certified home inspection report as a required part of the loan-application process. Most will only accept the services of a reputable, qualified company. Lenders realize that when the report is complete and reliable, it can save all of the parties involved a great deal of future hassle and legal expenses.

To help you decide on hiring a particular inspection service, you should ask the company for a list of references. Be sure to invest the time and effort to check them out. Determine the extent of their experience and reputation in the industry.

This written report will be as reliable as the person who conducted the inspection. Don't be misguided by a fancy dog-and-pony show or a high-pressure sales pitch.

A qualified professional is capable of submitting a formal report and can offer expert opinion or advice on any major corrective action that may be required. This person knows where to look for problems and how to detect a condition that may have an impact on your decision to purchase.

You will have acquired the knowledge to help you decide on the final amount you may be willing to pay for the property. With full understanding of the situation, you have reliable information that you can use to make an informed decision.

If, for any reason, you suspect the report may be unreliable, do not hesitate to question the inspector. If necessary, get another opinion.

It may appear to you that the inspector is being overly cautious or evasive in the responses given or the conclusions reached. Perhaps for any number of reasons you are just not comfortable. Then you are best advised to clear up any doubts or go on to another house.

It has become common practice for the sophisticated buyer to ask the seller to provide a one-year warranty on any latent defects or hidden problems that may surface. Be *aware* that some unforeseen condition can put a serious hurt on your pocketbook.

Requirements of a Property

Your lifestyle choice will dictate the size and the shape of the land. Will it be a small lot on a city street, a piece of suburbia, or some acreage off the interstate? In any case, each property will have conditional land uses and regulations attached to the land through local zoning regulations.

Unfortunately, some buyers do not understand the impact that certain local rules and regulations could have on their intended use. Your anticipated use of the property may be impacted by these local zoning regulations or by deed restrictions. These regulations could affect the manner in which you are able to enjoy the property.

Even though you are the owner, you may be limited or restricted by the permitted uses. Therefore, it becomes necessary to be very familiar with the inclusions as well as the exclusions in these land use controls. This type of information is available from the local building-code enforcement official or the zoning board office.

Stop in at the office of the zoning official and get a copy of the rules and regulations. Verify the zone and the permitted uses of the property.

Some examples of the most common permitted use issues include parking and storage of trailers or recreational vehicles; installation of a pool or tennis court; set-back dimensions that may affect the addition of a garage or other building expansion; the number of nonfamily members allowed to be living in the building; off-street parking and many other matters of concern.

In addition, you will want to be *aware* of the land uses permitted on the adjoining properties and in the immediate area. You do not want to be shocked to learn of the plans to construct a transfer station for garbage and trash, or some other similar facility, in the neighborhood after you have made a substantial investment.

Evaluate the probability that the community will sustain the test of time and remain in its present form. Go to the tax office and ask to see the history of the real estate and school tax rates of the previous few years. Have they changed or will they change? Is the town in financial trouble or is the tax base stable?

If you are working with a buyer's agent, you will be given reliable information upon which you can make an informed decision.

Identify all the current needs for everyone in the household and try to anticipate any changes that may occur in the foreseeable future as children grow, get older and move out, or in fact, move back in.

Consider those who may not be members of the immediate family but who could be living in the house and will require some space.

The size, shape, and condition of the building are most often the first issues that are evaluated. The primary concerns are usually the number and size of the bedrooms compared to the number of bathrooms along with the age of the building.

Is it large enough? If you need to, will you be permitted to add onto the building? On the sides or at the rear? Or perhaps another level up?

Do not accept the opinion offered by the seller. If it's incorrect, you will have little or no recourse after you own the property.

At the risk of being repetitive, ask questions!

Essentials of the Building

Begin with the basic requirements before expanding to the desired features. You must be as organized as possible to separate the absolute needs from the "wish list." Create a different written list for each category. This is definitely the most critical phase in the searching process.

By referring to this written list, you will stay focused on your priorities and avoid wasting a lot of time looking at all the "wrong properties," those that do not come close enough to measure up to your specific requirements.

Although you may be willing to make compromises in some instances, you should stay firm with your priorities. Do not accept any conditions that are not suitable or cannot be changed without a great deal of effort and cost.

Take a look at the sample list at the end of *Step Eight*. Prepare one that works for you. Even the minor issues should be listed.

Building Types and Styles

The homes that were constructed prior to 1940 are often labeled "older homes" in the language of real estate. These buildings are mostly located in the urban settings of many cities but can also be found in the rural areas.

Unfortunately, many of these homes have deteriorated to such a degree that they may have reached the end of their usefulness. And without a great deal of renovation cost, they cannot be made to conform to current building codes.

However, do not inadvertently pass up a property that may have the hidden potential for improvement. If the location is "right," the price is "right," and all other primary considerations are acceptable, take a good look. Think about. Each property should be reviewed for its own merits.

The Building Boom

In the mid 1940's and early 1950's, the heavy demand for immediate family housing paved the way for the major subdivision concept. With this new scenario, a large number of homes could be constructed in a very short period of time. The only condition was that each house would be similar, if not identical, to every other one. This method of using the fast-track construction process has been referred to as "tract housing." The new concept caught on and took place in many parts of the country.

Although the style of the houses constructed will vary, depending on the different locations in the country, the size pretty much stayed the same.

For example, in the Northeast the style was most often a Cape Cod or a ranch. With either style, the primary livable area was usually designed to max out between 1300 square feet and 1500 square feet. That was about the average size that was affordable to most buyers.

The layout is often three bedrooms and two bathrooms, with the master suite containing one of the bathrooms. The kitchen, dining room, and living room areas were proportioned to accommodate a family of two adults and two children. In some cases a partially finished basement is included.

Depending on the geometry of the lot a garage would have been included.

In many instances, these buildings are expandable. With some creative and inexpensive renovations they can usually turn into pleasant living conditions. When adding walls and other finishes to basements, these areas can be used for recreation, hobbies, home offices, and many other purposes. This can be a great starter home for most "newlyweds" and a first time buyer.

Very often dormers, or raised roofs, will work out best for adding space for the bedrooms and bathroom requirements. The new living area of these homes can then get as large as 1600 to 1800 square feet or perhaps more.

In most areas of the country, building size became accepted as the standard and continued in that role through the 1960's without much of a demand for larger homes.

In the 1970's, the creation of the split level and bi-level designs made an appearance on the scene. This style of building increased the size to 2500 square feet and in some cases up to 3000 square feet.

In the 1980's, the development of the subdivisions changed in response to the demands of the marketplace. The building lots were sized larger and the houses got bigger. Builders enlarged many of the rooms and added more closets and storage areas along with much larger kitchens.

Dens, great rooms, large entry foyers with vaulted ceilings, and, of course, the sweeping staircases became the new standard. The size of this house increased to over 4000 square feet and then some. Three-car garages were included. A fenced-in yard with room for a pool and a children's play area became a necessity. Don't forget the patio and the barbeque.

Wait, Get Ready—There's More!

The race for size was getting into a full speed ahead with no limits mode.

In the 1990's, another group of home buyers emerged. Builders now were required to construct "mini-mansions," aka "McMansions." The size of these new homes grew in excess of 7000 square feet. Many of them were built even larger. Can you believe it? Yes, you can. It happened!

This buyer wanted the biggest and best as an expression of their success and accomplishments—a very admirable characteristic, I might add.

In the mid 1990's, I had the opportunity to construct a custom-built home in a "mother-daughter" style layout that finished out at 11000 square feet. That gets pretty close to the size of a small B&B. The building includes 7 bedroom suites each with its own private bathroom. The "mother" side houses a large bedroom suite, a full service kitchen, laundry facilities, den, full size dining room, great room and of course a private entrance.

Other amenities include a pool, a BBQ, a few patio areas and 8 garages.

At some point, the size of these buildings gets to be just a little outrageous and border on becoming monstrosities. But of course this particular one that I designed and built is absolutely outstanding.

Using the words of Tom Bodett, "We'll leave the light on for you."

As you can see, there are a variety of choices available. With a little practice you can almost determine the overall size of the house and the range of years in which it was built, just by the style of the building.

Make the comparisons, refer to your priority list, and be absolutely sure to check your pocketbook. You need to know "what's in your wallet."

Reality Check

Well the good old days are gone. The inflated real estate bubble has burst. Now those big shooters are trading down—not up. Times have changed. You don't see a lot of the old attitude "just buy it, up the price and flip it."

It's no longer a seller's market. Serious buyers now have the opportunity to find a quality property at the right price.

Be *sensitive* to your situation. You don't want to create a serious problem for yourself, where you buy it but can't afford to keep it. There are some really good deals out there. However, be prepared to spend the time to find the right one for you. It may take a while to locate that "just right property." Don't be in such a hurry where you make a poor choice.

You can no longer buy a property, no matter what the cost, and expect to sell it at a profit. The demand for housing has slowed down quite a bit. It has become a buyer's market.

Lifestyle Choices

Have you given serious thought to your lifestyle? Have you decided on the type of home you want? Will it be a single family home or perhaps a two family where you could pick up a little rental income? Is it a condominium unit? Perhaps a home in a retirement community? Are you downsizing?

Condominiums (Condo)

Condo ownership involves both individual and collective ownership, whereby the apartment owner has individual ownership to a specific unit within the building and shares in collective ownership in the rest of the property.

The common areas are those both inside and outside the building proper. They may include lobbies, elevators, hallways, recreation facilities, parking spaces, and all other areas shared by other unit owners. These common areas are owned in common with all the unit owners.

The condominium association documents (condo docs) will describe in detail the bylaws of the association, which govern the permitted use, restrictions, and obligations of all the parties.

For example, some condo docs have restrictions regarding pets permitted in the apartments or even on the property or the number of occupants living in the apartment or the subletting of the unit and a variety of other rules and regulations.

Usually, the association collects the fees and assessments that are relevant to repairs and maintenance of the common areas. Be sure to ask the management company if any assessments are pending and if any capital improvements are needed or planned. Get a copy of the latest financial report to determine if any fees or charges have been recently assessed to the owners. You could be liable for any unpaid or currently due fees or assessments.

Be *aware* that getting a mortgage loan in some condos may be difficult if certain building ownership conditions exist that do not meet the approval of FHA certified lenders. Check with your broker.

Adult Communities

The primary requirement of this concept is the makeup of the residents.

In an adult community, there is an age restriction imposed on the owners and occupants. The norm is fifty-five years old and older. However, you must check with the association for any other conditions of ownership that could affect your decision to purchase.

In some instances, these homes are made up of single-family detached units. Each owner has a garage or two and usually an outdoor patio area. Different style homes with varying amenities may also be offered.

In other situations, the apartments are part of a multi-unit complex.

Ownership is similar to condominium ownership, in that a condominium association is involved in the management of the entire complex.

Read through the original condo docs and any subsequent amendments before you make the commitment to purchase.

Step Six

You must make all the arrangements for your financing ASAP.

Financing a Purchase

One of the basic requirements to making a purchase is to estimate your purchasing power and your staying power. A great deal of time and effort will be wasted looking at the *wrong properties*, those that exceed your financial capabilities. You must continue to remain *vigilant* of the importance of the financial aspects of buying and owning a property.

Do Not Overextend!

In most situations, a straightforward first-mortgage loan, supplemented by some cash investment, is used for the purchase.

Mortgage loans are available from a variety of institutions. Usually it will be a bank, savings and loan, credit union, private lender, state/federal agencies, or a few other sources. A potential buyer should inquire at a number of sources and speak with mortgage lenders about current rates and terms. Mortgage opportunities vary as the market fluctuates.

Credit Reports

Get a copy of your credit report and check for any errors or omissions.

The most frequently recommended providers of credit reports are:

Equifax   Trans Union   Experian

Fico Score (Fair Isaac and Co.)

Your FICO score places a value on your credit history. The formula that is used to determine your FICO score is made up of a few key factors, including the following:

Outstanding Debt (30 percent): How much debt do you have on credit cards, mortgages, auto loan, student loan, alimony payment, and any other personal/business loans?

Payment History (35 percent): How have you been paying off these debts? Are you regularly paying them on time or are you often late? Have you defaulted on any loans?

Credit History (15 percent): How long have you had the different types of credit? The longer you have a good record with the same creditor, the better the score.

Credit Mix (10 percent): A mixture of credit will produce a higher credit score; for example, revolving credit, which is made up of credit cards or a credit line from a bank, and installment credit, which includes mortgages, auto loans, student loans, insurance payments, and other regular installment payments.

New Credit Applications (10 percent): Frequent credit applications, within a short time, can lower your score.

A lender will consider all these factors and more when deciding on the approval of your loan application.

The FICO scale starts at 300 and goes to 850/900. Most people have a score between 600 and 800. Usually a score of 720 or higher will produce the best interest rates on a specific mortgage note.

The FICO scoring model does not consider age, income, race, education, marital status, length of employment, or whether you own or rent a home.

Get Pre-qualified

Your buyer's agent will assist you with this procedure, or you can try to use the services of a mortgage broker or financial advisor for guidance. You must know the price range of the properties you can afford to purchase and not waste your time looking at those you can't buy.

It is important to check your credit reports within six months before you begin the search to locate and purchase a property. If any errors appear in the credit report, you will have time to make corrections.

Get Pre-approved

Whenever possible, a potential buyer should ask a mortgage lender for a pre-approval letter to get a sense of the borrowing power. Pre-approval will also expedite the application process after a contract to purchase has been signed. You need to be *aware* of your actual purchasing strength before you begin the house-hunting process.

Mortgage Process

You will be required to furnish certain personal information on the mortgage loan application, which will allow the lender to reach a fair and proper determination of your borrowing capability. Have available copies of your W-2 statements from the last two years as well as current employment information, copies of recent pay stubs, current debt information, monthly expenses, financial obligations, i.e., alimony payments, auto loans, personal loans, credit card debt, etc., and checkbook and savings account statements.

Most lenders will only review an application for a specific property. Provide a copy of the purchase agreement. Although the criteria are generally the same with all lenders, the specifics that determine the final outcome will vary. Depending upon any number of factors, one lender may, and will, reject a loan while another lender will approve a loan for the same applicant. As you can imagine, it is not always a simple task to find that lender interested in your particular situation.

Mortgage Broker

In most situations, the best procedure for an individual to follow may be to apply for a loan through a reliable mortgage broker. The mortgage broker will have access to many of the different funding sources and therefore can arrange for a loan that best suits your particular circumstances.

A mortgage broker can assist with the preparation of the loan application and submit a request to more than one lending source. A reliable broker will follow the application during the process to assure a quick response. The service is worth the cost. If at all possible, get references from your real estate broker.

Buyer's Borrowing Capacity

The potential borrower provides specific information to a few mortgage lenders through the loan application process. Based upon the applicant's credit history, income, expenses, etc., along with other relevant information, the mortgage broker will determine the buyer's borrowing capacity.

As a general rule, certain basic ratios will apply. If you work with the following examples, you will be able to qualify yourself.

Refer to the (PITI) table at the end of this section.

One example to determine your borrowing capacity:

Use your gross annual income amount and multiply that number by 2.75. In most cases, the result is the maximum loan amount that may be available to you through regular lending channels.

OK, let's use a total gross combined income of all the borrowers at $75,000.00. Multiply this by 2.75. Your loan amount could be as high as $200,000.00.

Now go to the payment table and you will find the payment amount of (PI) for $200,000, at the interest rate of 5% for 15 years, to be $1,581 and for 30 years to be $1,073.

To determine if you qualify for either of these (PI) amounts, use your gross annual income of $75,000.00 and apply the following formula:

Take the gross annual income of $75,000 and divide by 12 to arrive at the gross monthly income of $6,250.

Multiply this amount by .28, the result of $1,750.00 is the maximum monthly payment for (PITI) principal, interest, taxes, insurance you can safely handle.

The annual amount for taxes on a specific property can be found at the local tax office. If a listing agreement is in place the taxes should be indicated.

The annual cost for insurance can be provided by an insurance agency. Convert both of these amounts to a monthly payment amount.

Add those amounts together and then subtract that total from the $1,750.00. The difference will be the amount available for (PIxx) principal and interest on the loan.

As an experiment, let's do the math based on $75,000.00:

Maximum amount applicable to (PITI) is.........: $1,750.00

Guesstimated annual real estate taxes:$4,000.00

Guesstimated annual insurance costs:$2,000.00

Guesstimated total for (xxTI) equals: $6,000.00

Divide by 12. You get $500.00

Subtract the monthly amount of   -$500.00

The amount available for (PIxx): $1,250.00

Now go to the payment table to determine where you qualify. You will find you fit in between a 15 year loan and a 30 year loan.

One More Example

Use the same monthly income of $6,250.00. Multiply it by 36. This amount of $2,250.00 is the maximum monthly amount you should consider for (PITI), which includes all your other fixed monthly expenses. So, make a complete list of auto loans, alimony payments, credit cards, union dues, health insurance, private schools, etc.

Total up all your fixed monthly obligations (let's guess the amount to be about $1,000.00). Now subtract this amount from the basic $2,250.00, and you arrive at the same $1,250.00, the amount that is applicable to the total monthly payments for (PIxx). Got it?

That's Amazing! How Do They Do That?

Now that you have completed the experiment of determining your borrowing capacity and you are confident you can safely handle the financial aspects, you are ready to speak with a mortgage broker.

Upon the presentation of a mortgage loan application, the lender will make a determination of the viability of the application.

Buyer's Purchasing Power

Now you must decide on the amount of ready cash or other valuable considerations you have available to make a sound purchase. Add the cash amount to your borrowing limits and you will arrive at the maximum amount you can spend to make your purchase at this time. In the event this total is not sufficient to satisfy the asking price established by the seller, you may have the opportunity to become creative with the structure of your offer to purchase. Learn about the PMM described below.

Types of Mortgages

There are a variety of mortgage types available that can be structured to best suit the buyer's situation. A few of the most common types are:

Fixed Rate

Purchase Money

Assumable

Veterans

Federal Housing;

You should consult a reputable mortgage broker for specific details.

Fixed-Rate Mortgage

This is probably the most common type of mortgage used. The interest rate is fixed and stays constant throughout the entire term of the loan. The borrower can set a budget for the mortgage payment and know that the amount will not vary.

There are two basic plans used for this mortgage structure: the fifteen-year term and the thirty-year term. Look at the examples provided in the mortgage payment schedule. Get familiar with the differences in the amounts. Obviously, the thirty-year term has a lower monthly payment amount than the fifteen-year term. However, you must become *aware* of the total amount of interest that will be paid in each case.

For example, let's use a mortgage loan amount of $200,000.00 for fifteen years at the 4 % rate. The monthly payment is approximately $1,480.00. The fifteen-year term will require 180 payments. Do the math, $1,480.00 X 180. You will get the total amount of $266,400.00. The $66,400.00 difference is the amount you will have paid in interest over the term of the loan.

Now do the same calculations for a thirty-year term. The monthly payment is approximately $955.00 for 360 payments for a total of $343,800.00 You will pay $143,800.00 in interest. That is quite a difference from the $66,400.00, right? Well, that's the price you pay for borrowing money. The longer you need it, the more it costs.

Now compare the two monthly payments. Which one is right for you? If you can handle the larger amount with the shorter term, you obviously pay a lot less in interest.

Purchase Money Mortgage (PMM)

A (PMM) may be introduced into the offer when the potential buyer is unable to obtain a loan, from the standard lending sources, of sufficient amount to make the purchase. In a situation where the seller may be interested in assisting the buyer with a mortgage loan for all or most of the purchase price, a (PMM) is structured.

In some cases the seller's financial condition and motivation to sell can be the deciding factor for a (PMM).

One basic example of when a (PMM) could be implemented is as follows. Let's say the buyer has the cash for the 10 percent or 20 percent down payment but for any number of legitimate reasons is unable to obtain a loan amount sufficient enough to complete the purchase. We now have a shortfall. At this point the seller, in order to make a sale, can pick up the difference using a (PMM).

Another example is similar in the basics, but the seller is in a position to finance the entire mortgage amount for this buyer. There are many variations to this creative financing that a buyer can explore. Don't be bashful. You never know what might happen!

Assumable Mortgage

In some situations, the seller may have a mortgage in place with a balance that the buyer can assume. Of course, the approval of the lender is required. If available, this could be advantageous to both parties. Because a lot of time is saved chasing a new loan, usually the transaction can occur rather quickly.

Veteran Administration (VA)

The VA program does not make mortgage loans. The agency will only guarantee a portion of the loan so that the mortgage lender has another level of comfort built into the mortgage. Qualified veterans can then obtain mortgage loans with little or no money down and at very favorable rates.

Federal Housing Administration

The Federal Housing Administration (FHA) does not make mortgage loans. This agency only provides mortgage insurance on mortgages made by FHA-approved lenders. The loan limits will vary depending on the property type and the state in which the home is located.

In reality, the requirements for the VA or FHA to become involved frequently changes. Be sure to check with your mortgage broker or you can go directly to the VA or FHA website for the most current information on these programs.

Questions You Must Ask a Lender

What fees will I be expected to pay?

When will I receive a good-faith estimate?

Will there be a prepayment clause?

If I sell the property can the buyer assume the mortgage?

Will I be charged points to get the mortgage loan?

Do I need mortgage insurance?

Is there a grace period for late payments?

Ask the right questions; get reliable answers

You can access a variety of Internet sources to obtain current mortgage rates and other mortgage information. For example you can go to Google or any number of other web sites and after you fill in the data sheet you will get a payment schedule for any number of loan amounts.

These are a good source for quick information. Try it.

Of course you will need a qualified mortgage broker to walk you through the application process in order to obtain a loan.

(PITI) Principal Interest Taxes Insurance

(PIxx) Principal and Interest

(xxTI)Taxes and Insurance

Monthly Payment To Amortize A Loan

Rate	4.00 %		4.50 %	
Term Amount	15 YRS.	30 YRS.	15 YRS.	30 YRS.
150,000.00	1109.53	716.12	1147.49	760.03
175,000.00	1294.45	835.48	1338.74	886.70
200,000.00	1479.38	954.83	1529.99	1013.37
250,000.00	1849.22	1193.54	1912.48	1266.71
300,000.00	2219.06	1432.25	2294.98	1520.06

Rate	5.00 %		5.50 %	
Term Amount	15 YRS.	30 YRS.	15 YRS.	30 YRS.
150,000.00	1186.20	805.25	1225.64	851.69
175,000.00	1383.90	938.45	1429.91	993.64
200,000.00	1581.60	1073.66	1634.18	1135.68
250,000.00	1977.00	1342.08	2042.73	1419.58
300,000.00	2372.40	1878.91	2451.27	1703.47

These amounts are approximate. You should check with your broker. Do the math to determine the total amount you will pay for principal and interest over the term of the loan. Do not wait to be surprised.

P&I payment schedules are available on Google. Look them up.

Understand how to establish and apply true market value.

Comparative Market Analysis (CMA)

Comparative market analysis (CMA) is a comprehensive guide for use in comparing a specific property to other similar properties in the same marketplace. The information is obtained from public records based upon real estate transactions recorded within the previous 18 months.

Realtors have access to the CMAs through multiple-listing services and use this information when working with a client.

Information provided in the CMA should include the following:

Active listings, which are agency-listed properties currently offered for sale. Be *aware* that the values placed on these properties are not always the most realistic. Sellers can arrive at any value they choose in setting the asking price.

Recently sold properties are usually the most reliable source of current market value. They have sold within the past few months. Many appraisers use these comparable sales, along with other considerations, when making an appraisal of a specific property.

Listings under contract are those that have not yet gone to closing. Although they are not yet considered a comparable sale, the relevant information can be very useful.

The listing of properties recently removed from the market is also another good source for comparables, because an opinion can be reached, albeit a guess, as to the reasons for the removal. Here are a few reasons:

remained too long on the market

the offers received were too low

the house is in need of repairs or upgrades

the seller changed sales agents

or perhaps just priced too high

As you can see, any number of reasons could explain the removal.

When using the CMA, be attentive to note the differences between the properties as well as the similarities. Choose the homes that are the most similar. Then make any adjustments to reflect those differences. Issues such as size, style, age, amenities, upgrades, and overall general conditions are just some of the areas to be compared.

Consult your buyer's agent for a complete understanding.

Property Values

Market Value

Value is an abstract word that will have many different meanings. The most probable price at which a property will be sold becomes the estimated market value. This estimated value can be examined in a variety of methods, usually with a series of comparisons to other similar properties. Appraisers can be a reliable source for providing this type of information. However, the buyer must make the final determination of the market value.

Fair Market Value

The concept of fair market value presumes that both the buyer and the seller are well informed of current conditions and that they are equally motivated to complete a specific real estate transaction. The amount for which a property sells in the free market system becomes the function of supply and demand. When that amount is acceptable to both parties in a true arm's-length transaction, true market value has been established.

The Seller's Value

The *asking price* of a property has usually been established by most sellers, from conversations they have had with their sales agent. The sales agent uses the current data available to arrive at an amount that is comparable to other similar properties and offers an opinion of the market value. In most cases this amount is a reasonable reflection of the marketplace, but unfortunately it is often less than the seller's value. Herein lies one of the pricing problems that buyers face.

Many sellers that have owned a property for a while have developed a certain emotional attachment for it and will place a dollar value on all sorts of issues, some of which have no bearing on real estate value. This debate takes place, and only after a great deal of discussion will the seller and the listing agent finally settle on the "asking price."

The Buyer's Value

The methods that should be used by the buyer to determine market value are quite different from those used by the seller. Buyers must stay focused and be concerned with *real* fair market value. The buyer's value must first be a reflection of comparisons with other properties of matching characteristics—for example, location, size, age, condition, etc.—that have recently been purchased. A review of recent sales can be made by a visit to the local tax assessor's office.

The Hidden Value of a "Fixer-Upper"

Can you handle a "fixer-upper"? If so, you can benefit substantially from the increased value as the improvements take place. In some cases, the work can be performed over time while you occupy the home. With some tender loving care, a "fixer-upper" could turn out to be the right property for you.

Before you make the commitment to purchase, be sure to get a full report from a qualified home inspector. You must identify the extent of the work needed and apply a reasonable cost estimate to the work. Speak with a contractor with whom you have some confidence.

The Buyer Sets the Market Value

Be aware of how you arrived at your opinion of value, and be *sensitive* to compare this amount with the asking price. Should your estimated value be greater than the asking price, you may have found a *sleeper.* That's fantastic! This could be your lucky day.

However, be especially *vigilant,* you may have found instead an *albatross* that you will regret owning for a very long time.

Assessed Value

Assessed value is the value placed on a property by the local real estate tax authority for the purpose of determining the amount of the current taxes.

The tax-assessing officer will place a value on the property using all available information. In many instances, the amount paid for the property at the last sale, if the sale is rather current, will have some influence on the final determinations made.

Usually the land is valued separately from the building(s). Any future improvements to the buildings may affect the assessed value.

The real estate tax amount is then calculated by using this assessed amount multiplied by the tax rate. The tax rate is a function of the local municipal budget. Check with the tax office for this information.

The Final Stages

So, you think you found the "just right property". Now what? I suggest you take one more serious look at your priority list. Prepare a "must have" list and your "wish list". Separate the two and allow for some compromising.

Rarely will you find everything you would like to have in an existing home.

Prepare a list similar to the one at the end of *Step Eight.* Place a rating on each of the most important issues. You must stay objective. When you have completed your review you are getting close to making the offer.

Step Eight

Prepare yourself to negotiate for your best possible deal.

Letter of Intent

In the event you have been working with your buyer's agent, you can take advantage of the recommendations of this professional. If not, you must rely on your own best judgment as to the seller's situation and motivation.

Present your letter of intent to purchase to the seller or the seller's agent prior to presenting a formal contract offer. Stipulate all your terms and conditions and of course the price, upon which, if accepted, you will agree to submit a formal contract. *Do not* express any level of enthusiasm and be especially *aware* to avoid making any references as to your motivation.

Another word of advice: *Never,* at this stage in the process, offer the full asking price. You should consider an offer that is 10% to 12 % lower than the maximum you would ever pay and go with it. Of course, your value should have been determined by you to be fair and equitable. If you have any serious interest in this property, you should not "lowball" the offer.

A low ball offer will not accomplish very much. In fact it could hurt you.

If your preliminary offer is too low, it may be perceived by the seller as a "trial balloon", a waste of time and be regarded as offensive. You probably will not even get a response.

However, if you do get a response, it could provide you with some useful and interesting information about the seller that may be helpful to you in any future negotiating sessions.

You may have learned more about the seller's financial situation, the timing for a sale, and of course the bottom line amount that may be accepted.

These issues may certainly affect the seller's decision to accept or reject your formal offer and perhaps make a counter offer that could encourage a real negotiating opportunity.

When you submit this letter of intent offer to the seller or the seller's agent, be sure to include a substantial earnest money deposit as a sign of your good faith and your level of seriousness. This deposit can't be held or used unless the offer has been accepted.

Also include in this letter that you are prepared to enter into a formal contract quickly, because you have the capability to close the deal. Explain that you have been preapproved for the amount in the offer.

Be alert and move swiftly to present this letter. Demand a quick response. Set a three-day time limit in your letter for the seller to accept the terms as written or respond with comments. Do not allow the letter to just sit there at the seller's convenience. Insert a "time is of the essence" in the letter.

Let's say you get a response. If the response is in the form of a counteroffer to the price you offered, your original offer becomes null and void. You can request the return of your earnest money deposit and further negotiations may now continue.

Okay, here comes the big question—how much?

Only you can decide on the maximum price you will ever pay for this property. Never, under any circumstances, tell the seller's agent, or in fact your buyer's agent, unless your agent is your exclusive buyer's agent, what your maximum price really is.

Let me remind you that these agents, except your exclusive buyer's agent, also work for the seller through the Law of Agency and that whatever you disclose to them can and must be told to the seller.

Keep your thoughts to yourself, especially your motivation and the price.

Do not go any higher than your established value, for any reason. You must not and cannot be influenced by the asking price or be intimidated by any of the comments you can be sure you will hear. You must stay absolutely firm in your position. Do not forget that you are the buyer, and without a buyer, there will not be a sale. This means you have some extra leverage.

You and anyone on your side should have a serious conversation regarding your genuine interest to purchase this particular property.

I would hope you have had the opportunity to have inspected other similar properties. And, for whatever reasons, you have zeroed in on this one.

Timing and motivation are very critical issues.

The Listing Agreement

If there is a seller's agent involved, there will be a listing agreement in place. If possible, get a copy and read through it. You are primarily looking for any items that are specifically excluded from the sale; for example, floor coverings, window shades and blinds, lighting fixtures, fireplace accessories, built-in shelves or cabinets, and any other such items that you may believe are included but are not a part of the purchase. Find out before you present any offers.

Final Negotiation

Do you recall somebody saying "it's not personal; it's strictly business"?

You must negotiate in good faith. Before you sit down to begin the "final negotiation," prepare a list of issues that you will label "deal breakers." You absolutely will not budge on these issues. You should also have a list of issues that you will of course negotiate in your own best interest but you are willing to give up.

Be sensitive. You must not get negative and point out a bunch of problems with the property. By now, all parties are well *aware* of the conditions, and that is why you are negotiating. Keep in mind that the seller also needs to gain a few points. Therefore, everyone wins.

Review your list of all the existing conditions you observed when you inspected the property. You did make the awareness list of those issues that are in need of repair or replacement, didn't you? Now use it.

By now, you should have had an opportunity to carefully review the home-inspection report, either the one prepared by your inspector or the report given to you by the seller.

How about the comments from your "Uncle Louie"? Make note of the items that may have been pointed out as "serious" and therefore costly to fix. Get a cost estimate for each item. You will need to use it later on.

Some existing conditions may be in violation of current building codes and must be corrected immediately. Many jurisdictions will require a current certificate of occupancy issued by the building code official and or the fire marshal prior to the transfer of title. This situation usually occurs when older homes are involved.

There may be some conditions that you are willing to accept "as is," of course, with a credit in the form of a price reduction. This is where your exclusive buyer's agent can be most effective. There should be no hidden agenda. Your best interest is all that matters.

Does the seller have a list of "personal items" that are not included in the price? If so, be sure to get a copy for later reference.

Seller's Motivation

What could be the most important motivators for the seller? Perhaps you or your buyer's agent, during conversations with the seller or the seller's agent, picked up on any issue that seems to be the driving motivational force. Think back. Is there something?

Usually the most important issue is the price. Try to understand the seller's situation and the listing agent's position. They are trying to get the highest price they can. By now, you must have understood that *higher is definitely better* for both the seller and the seller's agent, but not for you the buyer.

Find out what the other important issues are to the seller. Is it only the price? Is it timing? Are you prepared to close quickly, or will you lose out on this one because you did not get ready with your financing?

Priority Checklist

Ratings: Poor Fair Good Comments

YOUR MOTIVATION _____

SELLER'S MOTIVATION _____

LIFESTYLE CHOICE _____

LOCATION _____

BUILDING SIZE & SHAPE _____

USE OF THE PROPERTY _____

YOUR VALUE _____

SELLER'S VALUE _____

MARKET VALUE _____

IS IT A FIXER UPPER? _____

CAN YOU AFFORD IT? _____

ALL OTHER REASONS _____

All right! You completed the review of your priorities, and the overall consensus from everyone, including your *Uncle Louie*, is favorable. You are now ready to make the offer.

Step Nine

Gain the confidence you need to become a stronger buyer.

The Formal Contract

All right, you are satisfied that all the negotiations of the terms, conditions, price, and all other issues have been resolved. You are ready to proceed to the contract stage.

If you have been working with a qualified buyer's agent, you should have all your ducks lined up and ready to go well in advance of the negotiation stage. Go over your buyer's checklist.

By now, you should have an attorney on your team, providing reliable advice to you as the various legal matters came up. Your attorney will consult with you and your agent, if you have been working with one, to compile all the relevant facts needed to prepare the formal written contract.

In some states, but not all, a licensed real estate broker can prepare the formal written contract offer for presentation to the seller or the seller's designated representative. In this situation, the contract must include the attorney review period clause.

Attorney Review

If a real estate broker representing either the buyer or the seller prepared the contract, the attorney review period will be required. Three business days after the contract has been received by the attorneys is usually the time allocated for this review.

After the written contract has been signed by the buyer and submitted to the seller, the attorneys for both parties must review the offer. During this attorney review period, they will ensure that all the terms and conditions presented are totally acceptable to both parties. Either party can void the contract within this review period, without ramifications. In that event, all deposits will be returned to the buyer.

Unless the attorney for either party expresses an objection to any of the terms or conditions within this three-day time period, the contract will become legally binding and can be enforced by either party.

However, if an attorney representing either the buyer or the seller prepares the contract offer, no attorney review clause will be required. Speak with your attorney or broker for clarification.

If you included a deposit check with your letter of intent offer and the check was returned to you because the offer was not accepted, you will be required to provide another deposit check attached to the contract. Be *aware* that this check is at risk.

Vicarious Liability

In some states where vicarious liability applies, real estate agents should disclose to their clients the potential damages from third party claims. Clients must be made *aware* of the financial exposure they may assume under the common law doctrine of agency. The client may become liable for the acts of their agents. Speak with your attorney and get all the facts. You must protect yourself from this potential problem.

Step Ten

Now comes the best part, the closing: The American Dream.

Pre-closing

Relax; you are almost there.

If you have been working with your buyer's agent or you have read and understood the suggestions and recommendations in this guide, you should be prepared to close the transaction.

All the required papers to close should have been gathered and reviewed; for example, a survey, the homeowner's insurance binder, the title insurance, mortgage, and note, the certificate of occupancy, the building inspection report, and other items pertinent to your particular situation.

Make arrangements with all the utility and service companies to transfer the meters and accounts into your name.

Do not close without making the final walkthrough.
Do not accept the keys prior to the closing.

The Final Walkthrough

This final walkthrough should be scheduled to take place as close as possible but prior to the closing date and preferably on the same day of the closing. Set the time so that your agent and the seller's agent can be present. You must take this opportunity to make certain that the property is substantially and generally in the same condition as you expected it to be.

Determine if anything is missing from the property that you believe you purchased. Review the personal items list that is in the listing agreement. Make sure the seller has completed all of the obligations made during the negotiating stage. Should there be any significant changes to the property, you must speak up at once. Your agent or representative must be informed as soon as possible before the actual closing so that the proper steps can be taken to protect your interest.

Closing Costs

Now, the most important matter for you will be to make available the balance of the required cash, in the form of a certified check.

The check is usually made payable to the closing agent, in escrow. The closing agent should notify you of the amount needed well in advance of the scheduled closing. You will be provided with a copy of the breakdown. You must also have an extra check or two with you to handle other unforeseen closing costs.

In addition to the actual purchase price of the property, you can expect to pay certain fees and other related costs. For example; the mortgage loan fees, points, title insurance and homeowner's insurance premiums, attorney fees, recording fees, transfer taxes, real estate taxes, real estate brokers commissions, survey, appraisals, home inspections, etc. Your closing agent will be able to verify each item in a clear and comprehensible manner.

Real Estate Settlement Procedures Act (RESPA)

The Real Estate Settlement Procedures Act (RESPA) was first enacted in 1974 and has been revised periodically. Check with your broker or lawyer for the latest revisions, and visit www.respa.com.

The purpose of the act is to inform buyers of all the charges they must pay at the closing by requiring full disclosure to be given to the buyer, usually a few days prior to the closing.

You should have ample time to review the charges listed. If you disagree with, or do not understand, any item listed, contact you representative or your buyer's agent immediately!

Some of the principal areas covered by the (RESPA) act are:

Good-faith estimate of closing costs * Uniform closing statement

Mortgage servicing disclosure statement

Title Insurance and Homeowners' Insurance

You will be required to have both policies in place before closing.

Title insurance protects the buyer of a property and the mortgage lender against a claim of interest by another party. A claim may pop up from a variety of past circumstances that may cause a cloud on the title. The value of the policy is equal to the loan amount.

Homeowners' insurance protects the property owner from any claims that may be made against the property by a third party due to unforeseen circumstances.

You should speak with a qualified insurance agent to get the best professional advice. Shop around for the best price and terms.

The Closing

The closing of the transaction involves a meeting of all the interested parties. Usually in attendance are the buyer, seller, real estate agents, and attorneys for both parties. Sometimes representatives of the mortgage lender, the title company, and the holder of an existing mortgage note, if any, may also be present.

At this time the promises made by each party are carried out.

In most transactions there are two closings. There is the closing of the buyer's loan, which permits the disbursement of the mortgage funds by the lender and the actual transfer of the property.

The principal purpose of the closing of the transaction is the delivery of the deed to the buyer and the receipt of the payment to the seller.

The closing may be held at any number of locations, including the offices of the lender, the title company, the closing officer, or the attorneys of either the buyer or the seller.

Your attorney will review all the documents and when satisfied of the accuracy will ask for the signatures of all the buyers.

Upon completion of the closing, certain documents will then be recorded in the local office of public records. You will be given an original where appropriate, or copies, of the documents for your records. After the deed has been recorded, you will receive your record copy.

Be sure to obtain the keys, entry codes, garage door openers, operating instructions or warranties for any and all heating or A/C units, kitchen appliances etc. Also ask for any other items or information the seller should have available to give to you for your future use.

It's a good practice to change the locks, entry codes and access to any other devices that someone could have obtained. You can never be too careful. It's better to be on the safe side.

In Conclusion

Don't pinch yourself. You are not dreaming! You did it. You climbed all the steps. You should be very proud of yourself for a job well done.

Yes! You bought a home.
You are now a bona fide homeowner!

And because you followed the procedures and recommendations in this real estate buyer's awareness plan, you should be enjoying the results of a very successful home buying experience.

In summary, let me offer my sincere congratulations for your amazing accomplishment. You may have hit a few bumps along the way, but now it's time to enjoy the American dream. From all of us who have helped you find and buy your home, to you and yours, we wish you happiness in your success.

Joseph J. Pacelli

NOTES

NOTES

NOTES

NOTES

NOTES

NOTES

NOTES

NOTES

NOTES

NOTES

NOTES

NOTES